Community Helpers

Garbage Collectors

by Tami Deedrick

Content Consultant:
Marilyn McGuire
Los Angeles Bureau of Sanitation
Los Angeles, California

Bridgestone Books

an imprint of Capstone Press

Bridgestone Books are published by Capstone Press
818 North Willow Street, Mankato, Minnesota 56001
http://www.capstone-press.com

Copyright © 1998 by Capstone Press. All rights reserved.
No part of this book may be reproduced without written permission from the publisher.
The publisher takes no responsibility for the use of any of the materials
or methods described in this book, nor for the products thereof.
Printed in the United States of America.

Library of Congress Cataloging-in-Publication Data
Deedrick, Tami.
    Garbage collectors/by Tami Deedrick.
    p. cm.--(Community helpers)
    Includes bibliographical references and index.
    Summary: Explains the work of garbage collectors, including their functions, tools, and
training.
    ISBN 1-56065-730-8
    1. Sanitation workers--Juvenile literature. [1. Sanitation workers. 2. Occupations.]
I. Title. II. Series: Community helpers (Mankato, Minn.)
TD794.D42   1998
628.4'42'023--dc21

                    97-31544
                    CIP
                    AC

Editorial credits
Editor, Timothy Larson; cover design, Timothy Halldin; photo research, Michelle L.
   Norstad
Photo credits
Helen Longest-Slaughter/Marty Saccone, cover
Unicorn Stock Photos/Eric R. Berndt, 4, 18; Aneal Vohra, 6, 10; Martha McBride, 8;
   Daniel J. Olson, 12; H.H. Thomas, 14; Alice M. Prescott, 16; Paul A. Hein, 20

Table of Contents

Garbage Collectors

Garbage collectors keep towns and cities clean. They pick up garbage and recyclables. Garbage is anything that is thrown away. Recyclables are things that can be used again. Many glass, paper, and metal objects are recyclables.

What Garbage Collectors Do

Garbage collectors stop at homes, buildings, and offices. They take garbage to landfills. A landfill is a place where garbage is dumped. They take recyclables to recycling centers. Machines prepare recyclables to be used again.

Where Garbage Collectors Work

Garbage collectors work in communities. A community is a group of people living in one area. Many garbage collectors work in towns and cities. Some garbage collectors work in the country.

What Garbage Collectors Drive

Garbage collectors drive garbage trucks.
Garbage trucks hold a lot of garbage.
Machines inside the trucks crush garbage.
Some garbage trucks also hold recyclables.

What Garbage Collectors Wear

Garbage collectors wear work clothes that are easy to clean. Some garbage collectors wear uniforms. Many garbage collectors wear gloves. The gloves keep their hands clean.

Tools Garbage Collectors Use

Garbage collectors use garbage cans to dump garbage into their trucks. Some use their trucks to empty garbage cans and dumpsters. A dumpster is a large, box-shaped garbage can.

Garbage Collectors and Training

Garbage collectors learn how to handle garbage safely. Garbage collectors also learn how to drive trucks. They learn to drive trucks in all kinds of weather.

People Who Help Garbage Collectors

Many people help garbage collectors by putting their garbage in cans. Mechanics help by fixing garbage trucks that break down. Landfill workers help by covering garbage with dirt. They also help by making room for more garbage.

How Garbage Collectors Help Others

Garbage collectors help everyone in their communities. They help by keeping garbage off streets and sidewalks. They help by picking up recyclables. Garbage collectors make communities cleaner places to live.

Hands On: Pick up Litter

Some people throw garbage on the ground. This garbage is called litter. Garbage collectors do not pick up litter.

You can help clean up the mess. Make a plan to pick up litter.

What You Need

Plastic garbage bags
Work gloves
A team of friends and adults

What You Do

1. Decide on a day, a time, and an area to pick up litter. The area can be a playground, park, or neighborhood. The area can be around a pond or along a stream.
2. Walk or have an adult drive your team to the area.
3. Make sure all team members wear gloves.
4. Pick up as much litter as you can. Place the litter in the garbage bags. Have adults pick up any broken glass.
5. Help the adults take the litter to a landfill.

Words to Know

community (kuh-MYOO-nuh-tee)—a group of people living in one area

dumpster (DUHMP-stur)—a large, box-shaped garbage can

garbage (GAR-bij)—anything that is thrown away

landfill (LAND-fil)—a place where garbage is dumped

recyclables (ree-SYE-kluh-buhls)—things that can be used again

Read More

Handelsman, Judith F. *Gardens from Garbage*. Brookfield, Conn.: Millbrook Press, 1993.

Maynard, Christopher. *Jobs People Do*. New York: Dorling Kindersley, 1997.

Showers, Paul. *Where Does the Garbage Go?* New York: Harper Collins, 1994.

Internet Sites

Handmade Paper from Recycled Scraps

http://auntannie.com/paper/paper.html

Welcome to Recycle City!

http://www.epa.gov/recyclecity

Index